The SUGAR COATED TEDDY

Dedication

To Joyce and Bobby who were first to enjoy
The Sugar-Coated Teddy

To Bryce, Sharon, Judi Karen, Billy Boy,
Sylvia and Robbie

To Darren, Becki-Jo, Sheri-Lynn, Scott, Guy,
Dimbi, and Jeffrey

This book is lovingly dedicated by
Mother, Grandmother, Great-grandmother Cottrell

The SUGAR COATED TEDDY

By
Edyth Young Cottrell
Author of "The Oats, Peas, Beans & Barley Cookbook"

Published by
Woodbridge Press Publishing Company
Santa Barbara, California 93111

Published and distributed by

Woodbridge Press Publishing Company
Post Office Box 6189
Santa Barbara, California 93111

Library of Congress Catalog Card Number: 75-37441

International Standard Book Number 0-912800-25-9.

Published simultaneously in the United States and Canada

Printed in the United States of America

3

This book is the property of

Name:_____

The Sugar-Coated Teddy

Teddy, whose other name is Bear, was sound asleep. He had been asleep longer than you or I ever sleep. Much longer. He had been asleep most of the long winter months.

It is commonly said that bears hibernate. However it is not true hibernation, for sometimes the pangs of hunger awaken the bear, who rouses up and goes out on a foray, which means much the same as a human's midnight raid on the refrigerator. The nursing mother bear will make a number of forays while the cubs are in the den sound asleep. They are much safer at home when they are so small and helpless.

Far out in the dark forest, in an old hollow tree, was Teddy's bed. He slept close to the warm furry side of his mother. He was curled up with his little black nose tucked under his paw. He looked just like a big, soft fur ball.

It is really a good thing that he can sleep so long for most of his sources of food just aren't there during the winter months; there aren't any tender buds and leaves or green grass, and if he dug into the bark to get some sweet sap he wouldn't find any, for it is safely stored away in the tree's winter storehouse.

A thick blanket of snow covered everything — the dry brown grass, the withered leaves, the empty nut shells, the pine cones where he might find a few remaining pine nuts, the dry salal berries which would taste good to a very hungry bear; even the sticks and stones and logs that he might turn over and find an unsuspecting juicy morsel are all buried deep under the white snow.

The little birds and the animals which do not have a winter's supply of food cached away in or near their snug little homes may often go to bed hungry. Teddy bear did not have to worry about food. While he was lying quietly sleeping he did not require much fuel for energy to keep the body processes running smoothly, the heart beating, the breathing in of the fresh air with its supply of oxygen to purify the blood and to be carried by it to all parts of the body. Teddy Bear had quite a supply of fuel stored as fat under his shiny brown fur coat, enough to last him for a long while as he slept quietly on and on.

Then one day when the snow was nearly all gone, the sun shone very brightly. The birds began to sing. Little green leaf buds began to come through the brown earth and on every branch and twig in the forest. The warm sunshine found its way through a crack in the old hollow tree. It shone right in Teddy Bear's face.

The sunshine seemed to say, "Wake up, Teddy Bear."

The birds singing in the trees seemed to say, "Wake up, Teddy Bear."

The growing grass and leaves seemed to say, "Wake up, Teddy Bear."

Then Teddy Bear began to wake up. He opened one eye. He yawned and stretched. He opened the other eye. Then he yawned and stretched again. He felt so tired. He did not want to get up.

Mother Bear began to stir. She felt the warm sunshine. She smelled the fresh growing things. Then Mother Bear felt hungry. She was very, very hungry.

Baby Teddy was hungry, too. He was just as hungry...as hungry as a bear!

Mother Bear said, "Woof-woof." That meant in bear language, "Get up, Baby Bear."

Teddy Bear rolled over and crawled out of his dark, warm bed. The bright sunlight made him blink and blink. He stretched and yawned, and yawned and stretched.

Mother Bear started off down the trail. Teddy followed as quick as a wink. Sometimes he ran ahead. Sometimes he ran along behind. Sometimes he ran to one side of the trail. Sometimes he ran to the other side of the trail. He found a few dried berries. He found some little green buds. Every little bite he tasted seemed to make him hungrier and hungrier. It was good to be out again in the fresh air and sunshine. He remembered the many places where he had found delicious food, and the fresh water from the lake. It seemed that his capacity for food and water was unlimited.

Soon Mother Bear and Teddy came to a clearing in the forest. There were evidences that some people had been around. Close to the door of a cabin was an old garbage can. It was stuffed full. It looked very interesting to Mother Bear and she started for it in a hurry. Teddy Bear was about to follow her when a little breeze brought a scent of something very delicious. He pricked up his ears, wiggled his nose, and sniffed again. There was something very sweet. He changed his course in a hurry and headed straight for that sweet, sweet odor.

The nearer he came the more his mouth watered. He had never seen anything that looked like that before. But anything that smelled so good surely couldn't harm him. That is what Teddy thought, but he little knew how harmful some sweet things can be.

There on the ground before him was a big, black kettle. He ran to it as fast as he could. It was covered all over on the inside with something sticky and sweet, and some of the sticky stuff had spilled over the edge and had run down the outside of the contraption. Teddy Bear did not know it, but that kettle had been used for cooking maple sugar.

All that Teddy knew was that it was good; oh, so good! And he knew just what to do about it. He set to work just as fast as his little pink tongue could lick. Um...um...how good it was!

Teddy put his foot on the handle of the big kettle and climbed up so that he could reach the sugar better. He stretched — just as far as he could. He was having the time of his life. Never before had he found anything so very delightful. And there was plenty more inside if he could just reach a little farther. Umm, he had it! Oops! that was just a wee bit too far...

All at once, without warning, Teddy was standing on his head — right in the middle of the kettle! He kicked and grunted, and grunted and kicked. He couldn't get up and he couldn't get down. So Teddy just kicked and grunted, and grunted and kicked some more. He probably thought, "What a sweet mess I'm in." But that didn't seem to help matters very much. So he kicked a little harder and grunted a little louder!

Soon Mother Bear heard her baby's grunts. She looked. She listened. Then you should have seen Mother Bear run! She ran to where Baby Teddy was upside down in the kettle.

Mother Bear pushed the big kettle. It was heavy and did not move. Then she pulled, but still it did not move. Mother Bear pushed again — just as hard as she could. The big kettle tipped and then rolled over...

...before Teddy Bear could wiggle out of the kettle, and what do you think happened? That kettle started to roll over and over. Down the hill the kettle rolled. Over and over, down the hill it rolled — with Teddy Bear inside!

Mother Bear could hardly believe her eyes! There rolled that big black kettle down the hill — and it was taking Baby Bear with it!

Mother Bear ran after the kettle. Down the steep pathway she ran.

Bumpity, bump — over the rough path the kettle rolled. Bumpity, bump — the kettle rolled, with Baby Bear still inside.

Bumpity, bump, bump — the kettle came to a stop with a jolt! It had rolled against a big black stump at the end of the trail. The kettle had come to a stop, but to poor Teddy it seemed that everything was still going around and around. The path and the trees and the stump seemed to be going around and around. Even Mother Bear seemed to be going around and around. The whole world seemed to be going around and around.

Poor Teddy was all tangled up with the old kettle. It seemed to him as if he had been bumped all over at the same time. How he wished he had never seen that horrid old black kettle!

At last things seemed to stop going around and around. Teddy Bear stretched his little legs. He crawled out of the kettle. He looked around. He looked down at himself. How surprised he was! He didn't know himself! Teddy Bear had a brand new coat! In place of his shiny brown coat he had a coat that was tan and sticky; and, oh, so sweet!

. . . .

Under a big tree, far from the steep path, the black stump, and the sugar kettle, Teddy Bear and Mother Bear found that removing that coat of sugar was really a sweet job!

P.S.: It may be that Teddy will not have a toothache or...

... a bad cold from eat-ing all that sugar... because of his good health habits!

-The Author

Let us take a look
at Teddy Bear's health habits.

E. Cottrell

Teddy's Health Habits

1. A Good Diet

Fruit and
  berries

Vegetables:
  Greens
Tender bark
Mushrooms
Other tender
  growth

Nuts

Milk

**2. Tender Loving Care
Trust, Confidence**

3. Water

4. Fresh Air

5. Sunshine

**6. Outdoor
Exercise**

7. Rest

Teddy's Health Habits

What keeps Teddy Bear well and strong and happy? Let us visit him in his forest home and find out how he lives.

A bear's home for the spring, summer, and fall is in the lovely, open forest. Here he eats, sleeps, hunts, and plays. He spends most of his time looking for food. In stormy weather he finds shelter in a cave or hollow log or stump.

His winter home is called a den. It is very simple. It is just a place to sleep. It must protect him from the cold winds, the rain and the snow. It may be a big hollow stump, a hollow log, or a cave. It has only one room and that is a bedroom. There is no need for a dining room or a kitchen, because a bear just uses this home for sleeping. He "hibernates" that is, he sleeps all winter long. It is not a true hibernation. The big bears may make several forays to find food. A foray is much the same as a midnight raid on the refrigerator.

It is in this winter home that the baby bears are born. Mother Bear wakes up. She gives daddy a nudge; that is, she hits him hard enough with her big paw or foot to awaken him. And she growls, too!

He knows what she means. He gets up. He is so sleepy, but he leaves at once. He finds an old hollow log and crawls in and goes back to sleep.

The mother bear may have one, or two, or three, or possibly four, baby cubs. They are tiny. They may weigh less than two pounds each.

The black bear's cubs are not always black! One may be black, one brown, one blond, and one cinnamon colored, all in the same family!

Mother's paw would completely cover one of the little cubs, and the full weight of it would crush the baby. So you see why Daddy Bear had to sleep in another place. He is so big and heavy. It just isn't safe to have him around!

Mother Bear is so sleepy that she is soon sound asleep again. The little cubs' eyes are shut, like a baby kitten's, and will be for several weeks. They snuggle close to their mother. Her warm body and long fur keep them warm. When the baby bear is hungry he nuzzles with his little nose and nurses until he has enough to eat. Then he goes to sleep again, while Mother Bear sleeps on and on.

E. Cottrell

Eat and sleep and grow is all that little cub bears have to do. And they do grow very fast. By the time Mother Bear brings them out of the den they may be as large as a three- or four-month-old Spaniel puppy.

At first much of their food is their mother's milk. But they soon learn how many good things there are to eat — all around them.

E. Cottrell

At first the little cubs stay close to the side of their mother. As they walk along the forest paths, Mother Bear shows them where to find growing leaf buds; choice, tender plants of early spring; and new green grass. Sometimes she scratches the bark from a tree and lets the cubs lick the sweet sap. Occasionally they find a tender fungus or some choice mushrooms.

When there are warnings of danger, a low growl from their mother sends the cubs scurrying up a tree to a place of safety while she snarls and shows her teeth. Her fierce look and deep growls as she rears up and bares her claws send the offenders running for their lives.

Walking in the beautiful out-of-doors is excellent exercise. And it's more fun when mother goes along. After the little bears are partly grown and are not so helpless and easily hurt, Father Bear comes back and joins the family. Often he goes with them on their long walks through the woods, up the mountain side, or along the banks of streams or lake.

ECottrell

The tender grass and leaves taste so good, and they are good for little bears. They are chock full of minerals and vitamins that will make glossy coats and sparkling eyes.

The grass and tender leaves and shoots are like the spinach, cabbage, collards, and even wild greens like dandelions and pigweed that boys and girls enjoy.

Boys and girls who eat well have sparkling eyes and hair that glistens in the sunlight!

E. Cottrell

Under the outer bark of the tree is a layer that is soft and moist. The sap or food for the tree is carried through this tender, inner bark to all the branches and twigs. It will make the tree grow and make the leaves, blossoms, fruit or seeds develop.

It will make the little bear grow, too; and, oh, how he enjoys this sweet, juicy morsel!

E. Cottrell

Umm! How good! Mushrooms of many varieties are found in the moist woods. There are some fungus growths on trees and logs that are, like mushrooms, good for bears to eat. Who do you suppose tells the little bears which ones are safe and which are not?

A sweet tooth...Teddy really has one or more! How he likes sweet things! Blueberries are good, and good for baby bears! They are good for boys and girls, too, just as they come from the bushes without any sugar added.

Berries of many varieties are found on the hillsides and up on the mountain slopes, from early to late fall.

Apples are as good for baby bears as they are for boys and girls. There should be a modern "Johnny Appleseed" who would plant apples all through the forest for the little bears; just as John Chapman trudged through the forests shortly after the Pilgrims came, planting apple seeds everywhere. That is why they called him "Johnny Appleseed."

E. Cottrel

Bears can really smell wild honey a long way off. They are ready to risk a few bee stings for a taste. The long fur protects most of the bear's body from bee stings. But around his eyes, his ears, his nose, and on his tummy, where the fur is worn thin by climbing trees, there is very little protection. On these spots the bees make a direct landing.

Ouch! How it hurts! For awhile he keeps on eating anyway, as fast as he can. But soon the hurt is so bad that he must get down and find something that will stop the pain.

Does it hurt you when you eat candy and cake with thick frosting and when you drink pop? You do not feel the hurt like baby bear feels the stings but it may really hurt your body much more than bee stings.

Teddy heads for a mud hole, just as fast as his little legs can go. He rolls in the cool, wet mud. How good it feels! He gets plenty of mud on the burning bee stings around his eyes, his ears, his nose, and his tummy. Before long the pain stops.

But the hurt to our bodies from eating too many sweets stays on and on. We may not feel it at first but many a toothache hurts as much as a bee sting and lasts much longer. There are some boys and girls in their teens who have to have all of their teeth pulled out and wear false teeth!

E. Cottrell

Nuts! How bears like nuts! Hazlenuts are found in many places. Pine nuts are a favorite with people as well as with little bears, squirrels, and other little folk of the woods. Every area has its special nuts. The cubs climb up and break off the branches and throw them down on the ground. Then they climb down where it is easier for them to crack the nuts and eat them. What a feast they have!

E. Cottrell

Look, Mom! No cavities! Teddy's diet is good with plenty of fresh fruits, vegetables, and nuts, together with milk. The milk is mother's milk, served with tender, loving care — which is just what every little baby needs. Then, sometimes, there are unsuspecting morsels which Teddy may find under stones or logs or which Mother Bear may share with him — some things which boys and girls do not need, nor would even think of eating! Teddy Bear has a beautiful set of teeth. He has never even been near a dentist's office!

Little bears are good swimmers. How much fun they have splashing around in the forest lakes and streams. Like boys and girls they play in the water. They try to pull or push each other in and no doubt run races to see which can swim across the lake the fastest. When they get out of the water they shake themselves like a wet dog does. Their heavy fur coats soon dry in the sun and have an additional sparkle, like shiny clean hair.

E. Cottrell

Drinking plenty of water is as good for Baby Bear as it is for boys and girls. How good the water tastes fresh from the streams, springs, and mountain lakes. With all of his activity in the warm sunshine he drinks and drinks and drinks. Mother Bear does not have to say to him, "Be sure that you drink at least six glasses of water today, dear."

E. Cottrell

Bears, like boys and girls, enjoy playing together. Sometimes it is a very rough and tumble play. The hard cuff may really hurt, but that is a part of growing up. It is all good fun!

After so much strenuous exercise the little bears are all tired out. They are ready to lie down in the shade of some bushes along the trail and take a good nap!

The summer is over. The leaves are falling. The wind is getting cold. The nuts and berries and tender greens and other good foods are stored away in layers of fat and in strong muscles under the warm, thick fur of mother, father, and cub bears.

The icy winds, the cold rains, and the snow will soon be here. The ponds and streams and lakes will soon be frozen over.

It is time for house hunting. The cubs will sleep snuggled close to Mother Bear. Father Bear will probably find a hollow log near by. Through the long, cold months they sleep and sleep and sleep.

When the warm spring sunshine awakens them, the cubs come out of their den with their mother. They have had their first birthday while they were asleep! They are now "going on two." They are big and strong but still in need of mother's watchful care. They are much more independent now and often wander much farther from mother than last year.

They are hungry; oh, so hungry! They are "as hungry as a bear." And that is just where that saying came from, for bears are truly "nearly starved" after going three or four months with little food. They start out quickly, eagerly, searching for the good things they remembered from last year. And Mother Bear does not say, "Now don't eat too much, dears," for she knows that it will take much good food to replace what has been used during the winter to keep them growing.

When the bear "cubs" go house hunting at the end of the second summer, they will be looking for new dens of their own. For they are then large and strong and quite able to care for themselves. Then, too, Mother Bear may come out of her den with still more cubs — one, or two, or three, or possibly four, tiny new ones to care for. However, the big cubs, "going on three" will sometimes join their mother and their tiny brothers and sisters on their walks along the lovely forest trails.

Boys' and Girls' Health Habits

Essentials for Health

1. Fresh Air
2. Water
3. Food
4. Sunshine
5. Exercise
6. Rest
7. Loving care, confidence and
   trust in parents and in God

1. Fresh Air. We can live only a few minutes without air. Pure, fresh air purifies the blood and helps to make the brain keen and alert. Air is necessary for all the body functions.

The house should be aired every day by opening doors and windows. Absolute cleanliness is necessary to keep the air pure. No food should be allowed to accumulate and spoil. There should be no trash, piles of grass, leaves or the like, left to decay near the house.

Plants should not be in the sleeping rooms at night. During the day growing plants purify the air by using carbon-dioxide and giving off oxygen. At night they do just the opposite — they use the oxygen and give off carbon-dioxide.

The air should be free from smoke and other poisonous fumes.

2. Water. We can live only a few days without water. Nearly nine-tenths of the weight of the body is water. Food and oxygen from the air are carried by the blood to all parts of the body. Water is necessary for cleansing the body both inside and out. The body, the clothing, the house should be kept clean by the free use of water.

Drink six to eight glasses of water every day. Form the habit of drinking two or more glasses of water before breakfast. Very warm water is best to drink the first thing in the morning — not hot enough to burn but just slightly hot. It shouldn't feel hot as you swallow. It cleanses the stomach, stimulates the flow of the digestive juices and is a good aid to digestion.

Drink one-half hour before breakfast and also one-half hour before other meals; then you will not be thirsty and want so much to drink with your meals. Do not drink very much at mealtime, especially ice water, or sugary drinks.

3. Food. Good food is necessary to make strong bodies. It should be prepared simply from unrefined natural foods, vegetables, grains, nuts, and milk or fortified soy milk. (If soy milk, it should contain added Vitamin B_{12} and calcium.) These foods are absolutely necessary for boys and girls and for grown people, too. If eggs are used there should not be more than two or three a week.

Fruit makes the best dessert. Fruit, either fresh or dried, may be used as sweetening in many delicious desserts, and candies, and in making ice cream.

Eating for Health

a. Eat regularly — not one bite between meals, not even fruit!

b. Meals should be spaced four and one half to five hours apart.

c. Don't use sugary drinks, candies, rich cakes and cookies. They are not good for your health. Fruit makes the best dessert. There are delicious and healthful desserts made without sugar; many of them you can make yourself.

Most of Teddy Bear's sweets were fruits and berries. When he found a honey tree, the bees stung him on the nose to keep him from eating too much. How much candy, pop, cake, pie, cookies or ice cream would you want if a bee were stinging you on the nose? *None!*

That's just the amount you should use — none!

Cheer up! Try some of the delicious, wholesome sweets that you can make for yourself. One word of caution: Do not overeat! Not of sweets or of any other good food! Good health is the reward of being temperate in all of our habits of eating, drinking, sleeping, seeing, playing, and even working!

When bears are kept in parks and zoos, their caretakers won't let them have one bite of the foods that boys and girls like so well — sweets and sugar-coated cereals, potato chips, and refined and greasy foods. They are guarding the health of the bears so they will have glossy fur, bright eyes, and be keen and alert.

How shiny is your hair! Boys and girls should have shiny hair, bright eyes, and keen minds if they are healthy. And do you know what? They will also have good dispositions, and be happy.

4. Sunshine is nature's "disinfectant"; it helps to destroy germs, purify the air, and to supply vitamin D to your body when your skin is exposed to its rays. Raise the window shades and pull back the draperies and let the sunshine in. Windows should not be shaded by too many shrubs and trees. Bedding and clothing should be hung out in the sunshine now and then for thorough sunning.

5. Exercise is as necessary for boys and girls as it is for little bears. Walking, swimming, and playing; and, best of all, making a garden — all out-of-doors in the fresh air and sunshine. Outdoor exercise helps to make good blood, strong muscles, and keen minds, and to provide a good appetite for wholesome food.

Making a garden is extra special for boys and girls because of the added joy of seeing the miracle of life as the tiny seeds sprout and the leaves unfold and grow into plants that produce flowers, delicious fruits, and vegetables. The joy of working with the Master Gardener — God, the Creator — is health promoting.

The fresh fruits and vegetables have an extra amount of vitamins if they are prepared and served as soon as they are gathered from the garden. Then, too, there is the joy of satisfaction that comes from sharing with the family the good things that you have raised.

6. Rest is natural and sweet after a day of wholesome activity out-of-doors. Make sure that bedroom windows are open to let the fresh air circulate through the room.

7. Trust and confidence in parents and in God give a feeling of well-being that is followed by sound sleep, happiness, and health.

Delicious Recipes

Here are some delicious, healthful recipes; simple and easy to make. Boys and girls both like to cook good things to eat. Mother and Father may enjoy helping, too! You should be sure that they are helping you or watching you when mechanical or electrical equipment or heat are being used.

Banana Ice Cream

Select very ripe bananas (skins with dark patches). Peel bananas. Place in plastic bags. Freeze.

1/2 cup evaporated milk, concentrated soy milk or
nut milk
3 frozen bananas (see above)

Put chilled milk in top of blender, add 6 or 8 slices of frozen banana; turn to medium-high speed. Slice bananas and add one slice at a time into center. Be careful that bananas do not defrost. If load seems too hard for blender, stop. Slices may be frozen together (separate with fork). Blend until all slices are added. Consistency will be that of soft ice cream. Serve immediately. May be stored in freezer for an hour or two. Stir before serving.

Yummie Suggestion: soft banana ice cream may be served over fresh or frozen blue berries.

Banana Bon Bons

1/4 cup chopped dates
3/4 cup water
1 cup finely chopped nuts
  or nut meal

1 cup coconut
  (more if needed)
4 medium size, very ripe
  bananas

Blend dates and 1/2 cup water at high speed until fine. Empty into bowl. Rinse blender top with 1/4 cup water and add to date mixture in bowl. Stir well.

Combine chopped nuts and coconut. Mix well. Sprinkle half mixture of nuts and coconut evenly over the bottom of a small cookie sheet or tray — approximately 9" by 16".

Slice bananas into 1/2" slices. Place on layer of nuts and coconut in rows about 1/4" apart. Sprinkle evenly with remaining mixture, putting some between slices to coat the edges. Cover tray with foil or plastic wrap and freeze quickly. Serve at once or pack into a box and store in freezer. Yield: about 48.

Note: 2 cups of chopped nuts may be used instead of one cup each of nuts and coconut. The extra chopped nuts or chopped nuts and coconut mixture left on the cookie sheet after bon bons are removed may be stored in a small refrigerator dish and used again.

Barley Patty Crisps

1½ cups barley flour
1½ cups macaroon coconut
1/4 cup soy flour
1/2 teaspoon salt

1/2 cup water
1/4 cup oil
1 tablespoon sugar

Combine and mix dry ingredients in a bowl. Measure water and oil together in a glass measuring cup. Beat with a fork to emulsify. Pour over dry ingredients, stirring with a fork to moisten as evenly as possible. Mix well. Dip by teaspoon and place about two inches apart on ungreased cookie sheet. Flatten by pressing with a fork until quite thin and rounded in shape.

Bake at 350°F. about twenty-five minutes or until slightly browned. Turn off heat and let thoroughly dry. The length of time for browning and drying will depend on how thin the patties are — 1/4 inch in thickness is about right. Loosen with pancake turner and leave on cookie sheet until cool.

Fruit Bars

2½ cups rolled oats
1/2 cup fine
   whole wheat flour
1 tablespoon brown sugar

2 tablespoons soy flour
1/2 teaspoon salt
1/3 cup oil
1/3 cup cold water

Measure dry ingredients into a bowl. Mix. Measure oil and water into a measuring cup. Beat with fork until oil is emulsified. Pour gradually over dry ingredients in the bowl while stirring with a fork to moisten evenly.

Filling for Fruit Bars

1½ cups dates or
   raisins or half
   of each
1/2 cup water

1/4 teaspoon salt
1/2 cup chopped nuts
1 tablespoon lemon
   juice

Chop raisins and pitted dates with water in blender. Add salt, chopped nuts and lemon juice. Mix well.

Crumble a little less than half of the rolled oats mixture into the bottom of a greased 8" x 8" pan. Press down firmly with fingers. Spread filling evenly over crust. Crumble remaining crust mixture over filling and press down with fingers or fork.

Bake at 375°F. for 25 to 30 minutes or until a delicate brown. Cool before removing from pan. Loosen edges, invert pan on cloth-covered tray by putting tray on top of pan and turning over. Pat sharply on bottom of pan. Cut in two-inch squares. Yield: 16 squares.

Date-Bran Muffins

1 cup finely shredded
   raw apple
1/2 cup chopped dates
1/4 cup chopped nuts

1/4 cup oil
3/4 cup rolled oats
3/4 cup bran
1/2 teaspoon salt

Combine ingredients in a bowl and mix. Allow to stand for a few minutes to absorb moisture. Put paper baking cups in muffin pan. Spoon mixture into paper cups, pressing together and rounding. Make as large as you want the finished muffin to be. Bake at 375°F. 25 minutes. Yield: 12 medium muffins.

Fresh Applesauce

2 apples
1/2 cup pineapple juice

Wash apples, cut into quarters. Cut out core and stem and blossom ends. Slice. Put juice in blender, add about 1/3 of slices. Blend. Continue to add slices until all have been added.

Extra Special: Use this fresh applesauce on toast or waffles.

Spread whole wheat toast with peanut butter. Spoon fresh applesauce over top.

Apricot Nectar

1/2 cup apricots, fresh, canned, frozen, or dried
  (soaked in pineapple juice)
2 cups chilled pineapple juice

Combine apricots and pineapple juice in top of blender. Blend until smooth. Serve at once. Serves 4.

Apple Candy

3 apples
1/2 cup pineapple juice
1/4 cup frozen apple juice concentrate
1 cup chopped walnuts

Wash apples. Cut into quarters. Cut out core and stem. Slice. Put pineapple juice and apple juice concentrate in blender. Add about 1/3 of the apple slices. Blend. Add remaining slices gradually until all are blended.

Put blended apples into enamel broiler tray or large Pyrex baking dish. Set in oven that is heated to 250°F. Let cook until it begins to get thick. Have mother or some older person help you stir occasionally with long handled spoon. Scrape from edge of pan so it will not stick to edges and burn.

When as thick as thick jam take from oven and cool.

Put finely chopped walnuts into a bowl. Dip apple mixture with a teaspoon. Drop into chopped nuts, turn over with spoon. Put on cookie sheet covered with white paper towel. Flatten with fork. Cover with white paper towel. Let dry until firm. Serve.

For storage, pack in small boxes lined with wax paper. Cover. Store in cool place.

Apple Delight

1 apple
2 cups pineapple juice

Wash apple. Cut in quarters. Cut out core and stem and blossom ends. Slice apple without peeling. Put chilled pineapple juice in blender. Add apple slices and blend until smooth and fluffy. Pour into glasses and serve at once. A half teaspoon of finely chopped nuts may be sprinkled over top if desired. Serves 4.

Fruit Plate

1/2 small canteloupe with scoop of cottage cheese surrounded by black cherries, green grapes and strawberries with stems — mint leaves for garnish.

Banana-Peanut Butter Cookies

Turn oven on to heat at 350°F. Oil 8" x 12" cookie sheet using 1/2 teaspoon oil or solid shortening.

Measure and combine in mixing bowl.

1/2 cup very ripe mashed banana	2 tablespoons brown sugar
	1 teaspoon vanilla
1/2 cup old fashioned peanut butter	1/4 teaspoon salt

Beat until smooth and light, about 2 minutes. Measure 1 cup quick-cooking rolled oats, add to beaten mixture and stir in lightly with fork.

Drop from teaspoon on oiled cookie sheet. Flatten slightly with end of spoon. Bake 25 minutes or until nicely browned. Yield: 12 to 15 cookies.

Variations: use 1/4 cup chopped dates instead of brown sugar; use 1/2 cup brown rice flour instead of rolled oats; use 1/2 cup barley flour instead of rolled oats; omit brown sugar if desired.

Coconut Candy

1 tablespoon margarine	1/8 teaspoon salt
1/2 cup honey	3½ cups macaroon coconut
1/2 cup grandma's molasses or sorghum	1 teaspoon vanilla

Grease 8" x 12" pan with margarine.

Combine honey, molasses, and salt in a heavy saucepan. Boil. Stir occasionally at first, then constantly as it thickens. (Test: a small amount forms a firm ball when dropped in cold water. Temperature 250°F.) Remove from heat.

Stir in 3 cups coconut or enough to make very stiff. Sprinkle 1/4 cup coconut into bottom of pan.

Put candy into pan. Flatten. Cover with remaining coconut. Cut into inch squares before the candy hardens. Yield: 96 pieces. The pieces will each contain only 1/2 teaspoon of "sugar."

If you use a pan 8" x 8", the yield will be 64 pieces, each with only 3/4 teaspoon of "sugar."

Fruit Candy

1 cup pitted dates   1 cup macaroon coconut
1 cup raisins   1/4 teaspoon salt
1 cup chopped nuts

Chop dates. Grind raisins through food chopper using medium blade. Combine dates and raisins and mix well. Add chopped nuts and 3/4 cup of coconut. Mix well.

Form into rolls about 1½ inches in diameter. Roll in remaining coconut. Wrap in wax paper. Chill. Slice. Store in cool place in covered container. Yield: 36 pieces.

Variations: dried apples, dates, pineapple, apricots, or other fruits of your choice.

Peanut Butter Fudge

1/4 cup honey   1/2 teaspoon vanilla
1/4 cup molasses (very mild   1 cup + 2 tablespoons
   or sorghum)   soy milk powder
1/2 cup peanut butter

Combine honey, molasses, and peanut butter and beat until smooth. Add vanilla. Stir in dried soy milk powder. Knead a little after last addition. Should be firm, but not too dry.

Grease 8" x 8" pan lightly with margarine. Flatten fudge into pan by pressing with a rubber spatula until it is of even thickness and fills the corners. Cut in 1" squares. Store in covered dish. It dries quickly if exposed to air. Yield: 64 squares, each with only about 1/3 teaspoon of "sugar."

Note: may be rolled into balls about 1 inch in diameter and rolled in macaroon coconut or chopped nuts.

Creamy Bean Soup

2 cups cooked brown beans   1/2 teaspoon onion powder
1½ cups bean liquid and water   1/8 teaspoon garlic powder
1/2 teaspoon salt   1/2 cup evaporated milk

Combine beans, one cup liquid, and seasonings. Blend until smooth. Pour into heavy kettle that will not scorch easily. Rinse blender with 1/2 cup liquid and stir into blended beans.

Heat to boiling on a medium-hot burner. Reduce heat. Add evaporated milk. Allow to remain on simmer for a minute or two. Serve in cups or soup bowls. Yield: 4 - 1 cup servings. Serve with zwieback topped with slices of avocado.

Lettuce-Peanut Butter Roll-Ups

24 medium-size lettuce leaves
1/3 cup peanut butter
(Best with small to medium-size leaf lettuce fresh from your own garden.)

Wash 24 medium-size leaves of lettuce. Sort out larger leaves as you wash them and place on clean white paper towels to dry. Place the smaller leaves in a separate pile to dry — on white paper towels. Use 2 leaves for each roll-up. Spread the larger leaf lightly with peanut butter. Place the smaller leaf on top and spread it lightly with peanut butter. Pull into a small roll — a small amount of peanut butter on the outer edge of the larger leaf will hold the roll together. If there is difficulty with it sticking, a tooth pick through the roll will hold it together. Yield: 4 servings of 3 rolls each.

Finger Salad Plate

Sliced tomatoes
Sliced cucumbers
Celery sticks
Olives
Lettuce-peanut butter roll-ups

Other fresh vegetables may be used as desired, including cauliflower florets, green onions, radishes, carrot sticks.

Arrange attractively. Food should always be beautiful to appeal to the appetite.

Zwieback

Cut whole wheat bread into thin slices, place in oven at about 250°F and allow to dry thoroughly. Then let it be browned slightly all the way through — a light straw color.

Suggested Menu I

Apricot Nectar
Creamy Bean Soup
Zwieback with avocado slices
Finger Salad Plate
Banana Ice Cream or Banana Bon Bons

Suggested Menu II

Pineapple juice
Fruit Plate
Date-bran Muffins with margarine
Milk

An Index